free cities
CENTER

Launching an Urban Comeback

BACK FROM DYSTOPIA

Back from Dystopia: A New Vision for Western Cities
Steven Greenhut
Volume One

September 2022

ISBN: 978-1-934276-48-8

Pacific Research Institute
P.O. Box 60485
Pasadena, CA 91116

www.pacificresearch.org

BACK FROM DYSTOPIA
A NEW VISION FOR
WESTERN CITIES

By Steven Greenhut

VOLUME ONE

PRII
PACIFIC
RESEARCH
INSTITUTE

Why Vibrant Cities Matter

HAVING GROWN UP IN a placid tract-house suburb of Philadelphia in the 1970s, I had always longed for the excitement of cities – not just big, lively ones, but older, struggling "gritty" cities that had little to offer in terms of entertainment. As a teen, I'd ride my 10-speed bicycle to nearby Trenton, New Jersey, despite its boarded-up storefronts and ominous crime problem, or I'd drive my Datsun up the Delaware River to Bethlehem or east to Atlantic City.

During my freshman college year, while living in Reading, Pennsylvania, I was fascinated by Mary Procter's 1978 book, *Gritty Cities: A second look at Allentown, Bethlehem, Bridgeport, Hoboken, Lancaster, Norwich, Paterson, Reading, Trenton, Troy, Waterbury, Wilmington.*[1] The book provided a sympathetic take on some of the hard-scrabble Rust Belt towns that I grew up around, but which most people I knew largely avoided.

The book's black-and-white photography inspired me to traipse around Reading's row-house-lined streets and take pictures of its stark post-industrial urban landscape, including its miles of largely empty brick warehouses. Not everyone viewed this as odd. One *Washington Post* review of Procter's book noted "the romance of their smokestacks, derricks, mills and warehouses, seemingly built for eternity … against a setting of domes, spires, towers, gables and turrets, rows upon rows of houses and public buildings and spaces bursting with civic pride."[2]

For urban-planner Kevin Klinkenberg, "gritty cities" are a reaction to the sanitized nature of suburbia and an acceptance of the "imperfection, and perhaps even some danger, that lurked in buildings and blocks of older cities."[3] A lot of people relish those imperfections, although few of us want too much lurking danger.

There's something so interesting about these cities – and they offered endless possibilities. It always reminded me of the great urbanist writer Jane Jacobs' saying: "New ideas must use old buildings."[4] I loved to think of the cool business one might start in that character-laden old warehouse. In the ensuing years, American cities – including some of these gritty ones, at least to some degree – have had a revival, largely in part to the endless possibilities they offer.

However, there's a quality that's missing, even as upscale condos, hip shopping centers and corporate headquarters pop up around urban cores. Klinkenberg lays the blame on modern planning: "Our systems are largely built on trying to control every outcome from the top-down, trying to weed out any unpredictability or inconvenience and gradually decreasing the ability of the individual to make an impact through small projects or initiatives."[5]

That touches on my concern. Planning is important in every project. Obviously, private developers need to plan their projects, but modern government planners try to control every aspect of their new plans and forget that the vibrancy that we love in cities often is lost in the process. Many new urban developments end up having the charm and excitement of suburban developments or even theme parks, even though they happen to be built in cities.

The new mid-rise condominiums and surrounding shopping/entertainment venues that I see in Reno or Phoenix, for instance, don't look appreciably different than the ones I see in Sacramento, Everett, Wash., and Arlington, Va. It's like they've all been baked in the same kitchen or planned in the same bureau.

"Planning often fails because planners are disposed to treat cities as simple machines rather than the complex organisms that they are," the Pacific Research Institute's Kerry Jackson explained in a recent column for the Free Cities Center.[6] That's spot on.

I often marvel at the bone-headed features included in many suburban projects – such as a pergola and benches on a street corner at the edge of a Wal-Mart parking lot near where I live outside Sacramento. I've never seen anyone sit there because it's disconnected from any place a human being might be. Some county planner no doubt demanded that silly picnic spot, a few feet from a busy strip-mall corridor, because it ticked off some box (walkability!) in the building code.

Downtowns haven't been immune to such foolishness, either. In the 1960s and 1970s, urban planners closed some major center-city thoroughfares to traffic – only to find those streets atrophy and decay. The brain trusts didn't consider that the sidewalks adjacent to closed-off streets would become seedy, lonely and dangerous places once people stopped driving by.[7]

That once-trendy approach was a triumph of social engineering over civil engineering. Social engineering uses governmental planning powers to change the way residents live, whereas civil engineering builds the infrastructure that moves people around.

"Road diets" – embraced by planners and local officials in Sacramento, San Diego and other bigger California cities – are the latest example of social engineering.[8] To reduce accidents and promote alternative modes of transportation, planners are replacing street lanes with bike lanes. The results are predictable. Few people are replacing their cars with bicycles, and the ensuing rush hour gridlock is maddening. Instead of using light rail to avoid the delays, most endure the snarled traffic. Of course, putting too much focus on road and freeway building – something a previous generation of planners had advocated – has taken its toll on cities, also.

Commenting on the rash of urban freeway projects the nation embarked upon in the middle of the last century, *Vox's* Timothy B. Lee concluded, "By cutting urban neighborhoods in half, planners undermined the blocks on either side of the freeway. The freeways made nearby neighborhoods less walkable. Reduced foot traffic made them less attractive places for stores and restaurants. ... Those with the means to do so moved to the suburbs, accelerating the neighborhoods' decline."[9]

In some cases, the freeway-induced neighborhood disruptions were a feature not a bug. Princeton University Professor Kevin Kruse's 2005 book, *White Flight: Atlanta and the Making of Modern Conservatism*, details how Atlanta's 1950s-era planners used freeway construction as a means to essentially wall off certain (read: African American) neighborhoods and reinforce that era's appalling commitment to racial segregation.[10]

Some urbanists can't understand how such atrocities happened. Given the thinking that dominates in architecture and urban-planning schools these days, it's hard to imagine anyone proposing to build a six-lane freeway along an urban waterfront and demolish the interesting old neighborhoods and warehouses along the way. No one now chooses freeway routes based explicitly on a neighborhood's racial composition (even if new road and industrial projects sometimes impose undue burdens on existing poor and minority communities).

Yet, that's exactly what a previous generation of urban planners thought was best. Instead of seeing the answer as less government planning and more private decision-making, each successive generation of urban policy wonks promotes new and improved government planning.

Robert Moses spearheaded the creation of dozens of public agencies in New York City that funneled tens of millions of public dollars (primarily through bonds) into public-works projects following the Great Depression.[11] He was the ultimate master planner (at one point he simultaneously served on 12 city commissions), who planned the construction of major highways, parks, public housing developments and large-scale infrastructure projects.

As a 1939 *Atlantic* magazine article describes, "a Moses parkway means a 'ribbon park,' beautifully landscaped, usually from 300 hundred to 600 feet wide, through which a gracefully curving highway safely carries pleasure vehicles at 40 miles an hour . . . (where) there are no traffic lights, grade crossings, or left turns (and) commercial traffic, signs, hot-dog stands, and gas stations are taboo."[12]

Planners wanted to replace hot-dog stands, narrow streets and other messy vestiges of urban life with grand parkways that brought suburbanites into the city from Long Island. Modern urban theorists view the Moses legacy with understandable disdain, given its destruction of settled neighborhoods (slum clearance!). The urban-renewal philosophy put local officials – rather than individuals, operating within a system of protected property rights – in charge of development decisions.[13]

Urban studies academic Mindy Fullilove documents how these urban renewal projects destroyed many African American communities and led to some of the urban social ills we're still experiencing today.[14] She explained that in the early 20th century, African Americans migrated to the nation's cities, where – because of Jim Crow laws – they settled in ghetto areas.

Nevertheless, "they were able to develop functioning communities remarkable for achievements in culture, recreation and education." Many of these communities were vibrant places. Most were safe. By mid-century, though, urban-renewal programs began clearing away these "slums," with the end result being the dispossession of settled communities "and its accompanying psychological trauma, financial loss and rippling instability." It destroyed generations of social capital formation.[15]

Moses was the best-known advocate for these far-reaching redevelopment plans, described in a 2007 *Atlantic* article as the "godfather of sprawl" (which is no longer meant as a compliment.)

Modern urban strategies embody the opposite ideas – walkability, neighborhood cohesion and mixed uses.[16] Though preferable, this new sensibility still relies almost entirely on top-down planning – and gives short shrift to the preferences of the individuals and entrepreneurs who live and work in cities.

Today's planners are unlikely to bulldoze a warehouse district for a freeway, but they won't make it easy for just anyone to get a permit. They prefer subsidized projects by politically connected developers to market-rate actors. They're concerned about environmental justice in the placement of a new arterial highway or industrial facility but will also hold up the construction of worthy projects under the social-justice banner of stopping gentrification.

Jane Jacobs was the anti-Moses. She not only documented the havoc that urban renewal wreaked on New York and other cities but detailed an alternative vision of bottom-up development and decision-making. "As in all utopias," she wrote in response to the utopian Garden City planning movement from the early 20th century, "the right to have plans of any significance belonged only to the planners in charge."[17] That encapsulates the problem in *all* modern government planning.

In her seminal *Death and Life of Great American Cities*, Jacobs told the story of a new public-housing project in New York City that the planners were sure would be a great improvement from the "slum" that existed before it. Instead of appreciating the new project, however, the residents despised it – even though it included the park space and other modern amenities that the planners thought were so necessary for a modern, healthy existence.

"Nobody cared what we wanted when they built this place," one of the residents told Jacobs. "They threw our houses down and pushed us here and pushed our friends somewhere else. We don't have a place around here to get a cup of coffee or a newspaper even, or borrow 50 cents. Nobody cared what we need. But the big men come and look at that grass and say, 'Isn't it wonderful! Now the poor have everything!'"[18]

Jacobs continued: "(T)he principles of sorting out – and of bringing order by repression of all plans but the planners' – have been easily extended to all manner of city functions, until today a land-use master plan for a big city is largely a matter of proposed placement, often in relation to transportation, of many series of decontaminated sortings."[19]

She also pointed to Boston's North End, with its winding, narrow streets, cramped row houses and little shops, as the kind of tenement-packed place that a previous generation of planners wanted to demolish. I was recently in Boston and that's one of the city's premier historic neighborhoods, where throngs of tourists meander from the nearby Faneuil Hall marketplace and enjoy the Italian restaurants and nightlife. Thank heavens the planners never got their way.

My premise, in this short book and throughout the Free Cities Center, is that individuals should be empowered to sort out their own lives and officials should focus mainly on providing stellar public services (roads, public safety, education, etc.) To do so, they need to accept the kind of messiness that is fundamental to a free society and remains a reason that cities draw so many of us to their diverse, noisy and lively landscapes. New buildings can coexist with old ones. Variety enlivens the landscape. The market needs to work its magic. It's OK to just let individual property owners spearhead their own projects.

One final point: Urban officials have generally done a crummy job tending to their legitimate functions. When I promote the idea of gritty or messy cities, I'm not advocating for the filth and lawlessness that have overtaken some of the nation's greatest urban centers, such as San Francisco. Visitors shouldn't need a phone app to navigate their way around human feces,[20] nor avoid great public parks because they've been turned into homeless encampments and open-air drug markets.

Residents need to feel safe living in their own homes and walking in their neighborhoods. Transit systems should be accessible and cheery, rather than drab and foreboding. Parents – regardless of their income level – need quality schools for their kids.

Even as cities have built shiny, new subsidized affordable housing projects (often at unimaginable public costs, such as $700,000 to $1 million per unit in Los Angeles)[21] or permitted the construction of new skyscrapers and entertainment plazas, they have failed to tend to the basics. Building decisions must be driven by market factors, not government plans and subsidies.

One of the untold stories of California's government redevelopment process was the degree to which their central plans squelched the natural redevelopment process. Because those agencies had expansive eminent-domain powers, small owners stopped investing and improving their own properties as they waited for the big decisions from City Hall.

I once was the parish council chairman of an Orange County church that had inherited an old medical building in a poor, south Los Angeles County city. We wanted to renovate the building or build a new one on the site, but it was located within a redevelopment zone where city planners had free reign to use eminent domain (and where scandals had plagued the agency).

The city struggled to create a plan for the area over several years, so we ultimately decided it was too risky to redevelop the building on our own. We installed a new roof and left it as it was.

Cities should be treated as living organisms that reflect the goals and desires of the people who live and work there, which means accepting the natural process of growth and decay and providing property owners with the confidence that if they invest in their property the city won't come along and take it. Messiness, as I see it, means allowing that process to work – not trying to bulldoze neighborhoods and replace them with fancy but sterile planning-driven projects.

How Progressive Policies Harm Cities

THANKS TO THE NATION'S obvious political sorting, liberal Democrats generally run the nation's bigger cities and conservative Republicans often control suburban and rural areas. As a result, urban policy has become entangled in the nation's ongoing political grudge matches. Progressives portray themselves as champions of urban life and conservatives often use cities as rhetorical punching bags.

For instance, conservative politicians use progressive cities as the epitome of everything wrong with the country. Orange County's Republican District Attorney Todd Spitzer based his successful re-election campaign on the theme, "No LA in OC."[22] He argued his opponent would bring Los Angeles County's lax crime-fighting policies to that largely suburban region. It played on long-running disdain of LA by OC's more conservative residents.

There's a legitimate debate there, given the controversial policies adopted by Los Angeles County District Attorney George Gascón. A prominent "progressive prosecutor," Gascón chose never to seek the death penalty, barred his deputies from ever charging teens as adults and focused more on reducing incarceration than prosecuting criminals.[23] Ironically, Spitzer has called for a variety of criminal-justice reforms, but political campaigns rarely bring out any such subtleties.

And, of course, conservatives have a field day picking on San Francisco. A downloadable "poop app" that helps visitors navigate their way around human feces as they stroll around downtown received enormous attention because it highlighted the city's sprawling homeless problems.[24] San Francisco remains a lovely city despite its many problems, but conservatives routinely depict its street life as the dystopian scene from the movie "Road Warrior." (For their part, progressives love to portray suburbs – and Orange County in particular – as bastions of sameness, despite OC's and other suburban areas' vast cultural, demographic and economic diversity.)

Former Bay Area progressive Michael Shellenberger, who received much conservative support for his failed, longshot gubernatorial bid, is best known for his book, *San Fransicko: Why Progressives Ruin Cities*. "What kind of a civilization leaves its most vulnerable people to use deadly substances and die on the streets?" he writes. "What kind of city regulates ice cream stores more strictly than drug dealers who kill 713 of its citizens in a single year? What kind of people moralize about their superior treatment of the poor, people of color, and addicts while enabling and subsidizing the conditions of their death?"[25]

Ironically, even as progressives have allowed big cities to descend into disorder, they continue their quest to urbanize the country. As I wrote for the *Orange County Register*, "Despite a 50-year government campaign to urbanize our society, more

Californians are choosing to live in smoggy, hot, unexciting, and suburban inland areas far from the beach rather than put up with the high prices, fraying social fabric, and congestion of our destination metropolises. Few of the state's fastest-growing cities are urban in the traditional sense."[26]

In fact, San Francisco has lost 6.7 percent of its population since the beginning of COVID.[27] Well, the population isn't actually lost per se – former San Francisco residents have moved to suburban areas, to inland cities and to other states in search of more affordable housing, lower crime rates, less congestion and a better overall quality of life. Other hip coastal Western cities, such as Seattle, San Diego, Los Angeles and Portland have lost population also – although at a lesser rate than San Francisco.

Progressives blame COVID deaths and remote-work situations for the losses, but growing regions have dealt with pandemic deaths, too. Changes in the nature of work gave people the opportunity to live elsewhere – an opportunity many of them took. What does that say about the desirability of living in big, Western state cities? When they no longer must live in these bustling cities for their jobs, people are hightailing it elsewhere. These cities are exciting, vibrant places – but at a certain point the hassles become too much to bear.

During the Black Lives Matter protests, some of which turned into riots, city leaders largely took a hands-off approach as people smashed downtown store windows and, in Portland and Seattle, turned several blocks into "anarchist jurisdictions."[28] I've long complained about heavy-handed policing techniques, but the answer isn't to let extremists turn downtown streets into no-go zones. I see the residual results in Sacramento, where many businesses remain boarded up. Western cities' overly aggressive COVID shutdown orders also forced many successful local businesses to shutter. Almost all of my favorite downtown restaurants have gone out of business.

There has been some good news lately in San Francisco relating to the city's schools.

During the pandemic, parents grew increasingly upset as the powerful local teachers' union, allied with the city's school board, showed no particular interest in re-opening the schools – and no real concern about the lost educational opportunities especially for the district's poorest students. Instead of focusing on getting kids back to school – or at least educating them competently through distance learning – school board members spent their time on politically correct endeavors, such as renaming 44 schools that had honored such "right wing" figures as naturalist John Muir, U.S. Sen. (and former mayor) Dianne Feinstein, Abraham Lincoln and Paul Revere.[29]

The board also wanted to destroy (by painting over them) a series of historic Works Progress Administration murals painted in 1936 by Victor Arnautoff at the city's George Washington High School depicting images of slaves at George Washington's plantation and dying Native Americans. It spotlighted the nation's sometimes-sordid history, but the school board's hard-edged social-justice warriors found them demeaning.[30]

The board ultimately voted to cover up the murals rather than destroy them Taliban-style, but it provides insight into its thinking. The board also chose to shift the city's premier high school from a merit-based admissions system to a lottery system. Voters had enough of this nonsense and recalled the board members by overwhelming margins. One recalled school-board member referred to Asian parents with a vile racial epithet. In fact, Asian-American voters largely led the uprising.[31]

Even many progressives seemed relieved by the vote. "My take is that it was really about the frustration of the Board of Education doing their fundamental job," Mayor London Breed said, in a characteristically understated way. "And that is to make sure that our children are getting educated, that they get back into the classroom. And that did not occur. They were focusing on other things that were clearly a distraction."[32]

In my view, that's the key lesson here. Even in the nation's (arguably) most progressive big city, voters expect school board members and other elected officials to focus on the fundamentals of their job of educating students, rather than to use the posts to make far-reaching political statements. Then in the June 7 primary, San Franciscans recalled, by a 55-percent to 45-percent margin, District Attorney Chesa Boudin, who has gone far beyond Los Angeles District Attorney George Gascón in promoting a political agenda at the expense of a prosecutor's prime job of prosecuting crime.[33]

"We all agree that we need real criminal justice reform and police accountability now," the recall petition explains. "Chesa Boudin isn't delivering either priority — and since he took office, burglaries, car break-ins, homicides and overdose-related deaths are at a crisis level. Boudin is not keeping San Francisco safe. He refuses to adequately prosecute criminals and fails to take the drug dealing crisis seriously."[34]

But the real problem was that Boudin used his position primarily to lobby for vast social changes – rather than focusing on prosecuting criminals. The lesson from the June DA recall is the same one as the February school-board recall: Even the nation's most-liberal voters expect their elected officials to tend to the basics rather than spend their time on ideological flights of fancy. After the Boudin recall, Orange County DA Spitzer offered perhaps the best observation: "The progressives just took it too far...they went too far, too fast. There are things we can find common ground on," he told the *Orange County Register*.[35] Even in San Francisco, voters have limits.

This is good news. Instead of simply bashing the city, conservatives ought to celebrate local efforts to refocus the city's governance. I agree with conservative David French, who wrote following the board recall: "As a matter of governance, Tuesday's recall was an example of local citizens asserting local control. ... It represented the triumph of reason over radicalism."[36]

Four hundred miles south, in Anaheim, residents of a decidedly more conservative city also are finding ways to push the political focus back on the nuts-and-bolts of municipal governance and away from counterproductive political inertia. For years, Anaheim officials have showered large corporate players – the Angels baseball team, the Walt Disney Co. and nearby resorts – with subsidies, tax breaks and other special privileges.

Local activists had long complained that community concerns – safe streets, better schools, mobility – had taken a back seat to the city's quest for tourist dollars and national standing. Amid a federal investigation into the unseemly planned sale of the city owned Angel Stadium to a development group controlled by the team's owner, the city's entire political establishment is crumbling. In the face of allegations that he provided confidential information to the Angels as he sought a large campaign donation, Mayor Harry Sidhu resigned from office (but denied any wrongdoing and has not been charged with any crime).[37] It's a complex and sordid tale but suffice it to say that Anaheim's angry residents seem poised to take back their city from a failed political machine. The advocates for these policies weren't progressives, but they were as out of touch as their San Francisco counterparts.

The Pacific Research Institute's focus in the Free Cities Center is not politics, but public policy. What can we do as Westerners to help our biggest cities thrive and prosper? Yet we can't implement better policies without better politicians. In the past, under the leadership of former mayor and councilman, Tom Tait, Anaheim had embraced a freedom-friendly set of policies that prioritized property rights and the provision of quality public services. Ultimately, politicians funded by well-heeled corporate interests derailed the city's freedom experiment.[38] That experiment, however short lived, is one impetus for this project. Cities can become better places by letting individuals rather politicians lead the way.

The work of reviving our cities needn't be the job of one party or the other. It requires a new consensus – and sometimes the changes will come through intra-party power shifts. But most big cities are run by progressives – and the policies they have championed have largely been disastrous.

Taking Our Streets Back from the Homeless

THE SURGE IN HOMELESSNESS throughout California has become such a hot-button topic that it has been featured in virtually every campaign mailer I've received this season. The numbers tell a dismal story, but the visibility of the problem has put it on the political radar screen.

In 2020, California had 161,548 homeless people living here, or 28 percent of the nation's homeless, and the highest rate of unsheltered people at 70.4 percent. The state accounted for 51 percent of the nation's homeless population and the largest increase from the previous year.[39]

Recent data reporting since then has shown some pockets of improvement but mostly bad news:

While San Francisco showed a 15-percent drop in homeless, every other San Francisco Bay Area county except for Sonoma saw significant spikes in the number of people living on the streets:

- Contra Costa County saw a 35 percent increase
- Alameda County increased 22 percent

- Marin County increased 8 percent
- Santa Clara increased 3 percent
- The city of Oakland grew 24 percent

San Francisco officials credit their success on a dramatic increase in the number of available shelter beds, although such temporary fixes are not making a dent in the fundamental problem.[40]

Some communities that invested heavily in shelter construction (even at exorbitant costs) are seeing fewer people living on the streets. "The number of chronically homeless individuals in shelters increased by 49 percent between 2020 and 2021, which could mean that shelters are doing a good job targeting those who have been on the streets the longest," according to the Public Policy Institute of California.[41]

Recent reports from elsewhere in California show little room for encouragement. Homelessness grew 9 percent in San Diego according to the latest figures, and 31 percent in the city of Oceanside.[42] Sacramento's homeless population has increased 67 percent since 2019.[43]

Los Angeles' 2022 homeless count, delayed because of the Omicron outbreak, will be released in September, but the number of deaths among homeless people has soared. The news isn't particularly encouraging overall, although San Francisco's slight progress suggests that public pressure in the face of sprawling tent cities can at least force city officials to act – and rapid shelter construction can boost needed emergency accommodations.

And while homelessness is not primarily a housing problem, the state's outrageously high real-estate prices only exacerbate the problem. Jim Palmer, president of the Orange County Rescue Mission, told the Free Cities Center that 87 percent of the homeless people his non-profit group assists self-identify as having a mental-health disorder or substance-abuse addiction.[44]

That number is shocking, especially given that not everyone with such problems will admit to them – and it only applies to the people who have sought services from the mission. The actual percentage is certainly higher when one considers the many people living under bridges and in park areas who don't have the wherewithal or interest in seeking help.

A new study by the Rand Center for Housing and Homelessness found that more than two-thirds of the Los Angeles area homeless people it surveyed would reject group shelter arrangements.[45] As the *Los Angeles Times* reported, the city's mayoral candidates have all championed shelter construction – with candidates outbidding each other on the number of new beds that they are promising, as the city enforces a new anti-camping ordinance.[46]

That disconnect points to the limits of any temporary shelter solution.[47] The surveyed homeless people dislike curfews and limits on drug and alcohol use and are concerned about privacy and theft.

Such concerns are driving advocates of a Housing First policy that provides homeless people with no-strings-attached units.

According to the California Housing and Community Development Agency:

> Housing First is an approach to serving people experiencing homelessness that recognizes a homeless person must first be able to access

a decent, safe place to live, that does not limit length of stay (permanent housing), before stabilizing, improving health, reducing harmful behaviors, or increasing income. … (A)nyone experiencing homelessness should be connected to a permanent home as quickly as possible, and programs should remove barriers to accessing the housing, *like requirements for sobriety or absence of criminal history* (italics added).[48]

The approach has been a failure. "(I)t appears to attract more people from outside the homeless system, or keeps them in the homelessness system, because they are drawn to the promise of a permanent and usually rent-free room," reports the market-oriented Cicero Institute. It found that "cities have to build 10 … beds to remove a single homeless person from the street, since the vast majority of such units go to people who would not have been permanently homeless."[49] Nevertheless, this is the policy approach embraced by our state and its biggest cities.

Given that government contracting rules and inefficiencies force cities to spend hundreds of thousands of dollars per unit for permanent housing, available funding is insufficient.

Housing First approaches often result in addicts dying alone in their private units, Palmer explains.[50] There's no easy way to fix the homeless problem that avoids the toughest issues: getting people the mental health and addiction help that they need so they can live independent and productive lives.

California Gov. Gavin Newsom has proposed the Community Assistance, Recovery and Empowerment (CARE)

Court, which would allow judges to "sentence" homeless people to a court-ordered year-long treatment plan of 12 months (with a possibility for an additional year).[51]

Some California counties already have a similar homeless court system designed to send low-level homeless offenders to treatment facilities rather than jail, but the idea is running up against political obstacles. The first is California's Proposition 47, the 2014 initiative that reclassifies certain drug and theft offenses from felonies to misdemeanors.[52]

By reducing the consequences for thefts up to $950, Prop 47 makes it easier for homeless people to fund their drug habits without having to face a judge. Prosecutors lost their leverage to force these offenders into the kind of treatment programs preferred by the homeless courts. Homeless addicts often just stay on the streets and commit thefts as needed.

Newsom's plan also has met opposition from homeless activists, who bizarrely treat homeless people as a political interest group. "Instead of allocating vast sums of money towards establishing an unproven system of court-ordered treatment that does not guarantee housing, the state should expend its resources on a proven solution to homelessness for people living with mental health disabilities: guaranteed housing with voluntary services," according to a letter from several civil-rights groups opposing the enabling legislation.[53]

Such opposition reminds me of a point that Palmer made in a recent interview. If cities find a few homeless people in a public park, it's relatively easy to remove them and find them housing and other services. Once that park becomes a de facto tent city, the residents begin making demands and often get support from these kinds of activist groups. Then it's nearly impossible – at least without costly litigation and enormous delays – to remove the tents, old RVs and squatters. It doesn't help anyone.

The letter, however, spotlights how deeply these homeless activists have embraced the Housing First philosophy. Guaranteed permanent housing without strings attached is their go-to solution, yet that approach is doomed to failure. Meanwhile, they argue that the CARE Court is "antithetical to recovery principles, which are based on self-determination and self-direction."[54]

Our society rightly makes it difficult for the government to deprive people of their liberties unless they've committed a crime. Being schizophrenic is not a crime, so what happens when people with debilitating mental disorders are left to roam the streets? They can't realistically exert their self-determination and self-direction if they are dealing with those conditions. It's nearly impossible to convince them to leave the streets. It doesn't help that their self-appointed advocates refuse to recognize that conundrum.

This dilemma points to a 1967 law signed by Gov. Ronald Reagan. Called the Lanterman-Petris-Short Act, it "put an end to the inappropriate and often indefinite institutionalization of people with mental illnesses and developmental disabilities," according to *CALMatters*. "It also provided them with legal protections, such as the now-familiar rules in California limiting involuntary holds on people deemed a danger to themselves or others to 72 hours."[55] That legislation is perfectly understandable given the conditions in the state's mental hospitals – and the coercive tactics that officials had used to institutionalize people (and often for questionable reasons). But it did impose an obstacle for removing mentally unstable people from the streets.

There are no easy solutions, but the state should embrace a policy of triage. It must differentiate between homeless people whose problems are fundamentally financial (not enough money to rent an affordable apartment), those who need help to deal with their addictions and, finally, those who are not mentally competent to decide anything.

Western states and cities must fess up about the degree to which their land-use regulations have exacerbated the homelessness problem by making affordable housing such a scarcity – and recognize the limits of government subsidies and spending. They also need to rely more heavily on non-profit groups such as the Rescue Mission, which have decades of experience in providing compassionate aid to the homeless. State officials need to rethink their opposition to funding religious-based organizations, given that these groups also have long track records in helping homeless people address their problems and get back on their feet.

Finally, state officials must give up orthodoxies like Housing First, which are born out of ideologies, and focus instead on practical solutions. The Free Cities Center is committed to finding such solutions that treat homeless people in a humane way – but that also prioritize the needs of urban residents who have a right to safely enjoy their homes, streets and communities. No one should have a right to turn a city park into a war zone.

Making Housing Affordable Again

THE RAW NUMBERS ARE almost unfathomable. The median price for a single-family home in the entire state of California topped $850,000 in April 2022 – a figure that includes average costs even in lower-demand inland cities and rural areas. In Washington state, the price topped $666,000. In Oregon, it was $519,000. In Idaho, a top destination for California refugees, the median home price hit $512,000.[56] One national survey named Boise the least-affordable metro area in the nation after factoring that region's relatively low median-family income. That's the main reason Idahoans have become angry about the influx of Californians, who head to Idaho with sacks of cash after selling their tract houses.[57]

The situation is particularly severe in coastal regions. The median home price in Orange County recently topped $1 million. The median price topped $1.6 million in Santa Clara County – a boost of 14 percent since last year.[58] It was common for homes to receive dozens of offers and desperate homebuyers writing pathetic notes to sellers hoping that they would choose their bid.

The problem is more severe in the West because of the elevated price tags. The median price of a home in Texas has soared but remains at an enviable $376,000. Even in high-cost New Jersey, the median price is a manageable $433,000.[59] In my wife's hometown in rural Pennsylvania, one can still buy a handsome, 2,000 square-foot brick house for $115,000, based on a recent perusal of Realtor.com.[60]

I bought my first house in California in 1999 in the Los Angeles County suburb of Diamond Bar for what seemed like a fortune at the time, $217,000. Twenty-three years later, Zillow estimates that ordinary 1960s tract house's value at more than $1 million, or more than $500 a square foot. Based on inflation alone, its value ought to be around $380,000.[61] Something has gone wrong with the housing market.

For more detail, I consulted the California Association of Realtors' housing affordability index, which evaluates the percentage of households that can afford a median-priced home. That's the best calculator, given that a quadrupling of home prices wouldn't matter that much if median incomes had increased fourfold, also. From 1999 to 2022, however, median income in California essentially doubled – from $47,500 to $99,000.[62]

In the first quarter of 2022, only 24 percent of Californians could buy a median-priced home in their city and only 47 percent of Americans nationwide could do so. In Alameda County (the Oakland area), only 17 percent of residents could afford a median-priced home, and just 12 percent could in Santa Barbara County. A family needs an annual income of $435,000 in San Mateo County to buy a typical home. And buyers throughout the state need six-figure down payments.[63]

These unapproachable price points, also reflected in soaring rent prices, disrupt the stability of urban communities. They force people to work longer hours, promote less neighborhood cohesion and create a society of renters. There's nothing wrong with renting, but homebuyers tend to settle into their neighborhoods, get more involved in their communities and stay much longer. Rising prices create pressure for political "solutions" such as rent control that exacerbate the problem by discouraging investment in new rental housing.[64]

""Homeowners are more likely to participate in local elections, civic groups and neighborhood organizations than are renters," the Urban Institute notes.[65] "Housing can be an essential tool for upward mobility, giving families a strong foundation to move out of poverty," the institute adds.[66] Homeownership helps people build credit and equity and the social skills that help build a prosperous life.

This dramatic affordability shift has happened relatively quickly. After the latest housing bust, I purchased a rental house in a settled neighborhood of central Stockton, Calif. for $78,000. It's a nice bungalow on a leafy urban street – the kind of middle-class house that is common in that gritty, blue-collar city. Zillow pegs its current value at nearly $400,000, making it off limits to most people in a city with a median income of $41,000. Obviously, salaries there haven't increased fivefold over the last 13 years. Most everyone in that neighborhood now is a renter.

So what happened?

One can find myriad economic analyses that look at deep economic trends, inflation rates, Federal Reserve policies and demographic changes. Then the pandemic created an even larger and more rapid surge in prices. Harvard University's Joint Center for Housing Studies argued that COVID-19 caused builders to slow down home construction and discouraged potential sellers from listing their properties. It also noted a shift in family income toward housing, as people were stuck in their homes and more willing to invest in them. The pandemic also sparked second-home buying, as people could now work from remote locations. Interest rates remained at historic lows.[67]

But there's more to the home price hikes than pandemic policies. The most obvious problem is an imbalance in supply and demand. For years, Western states – and California in particular – have imposed regulatory policies that constrict new home construction or incentivize builders to construct only luxury products.[68]

Today's policymakers focus largely on building new affordable (and subsidized) units, but the real solution involves allowing the construction of all types of housing everywhere. Lower- and middle-income buyers don't typically buy new homes, but they can buy the "used" homes that wealthier buyers sell as they move up the housing ladder to newer and fancier digs.

Bottom line: States and localities have succumbed to political pressure to limit new construction to placate existing homeowners who complain about congestion and traffic and seek open space. The result is an artificially reduced housing supply.

The Manhattan Institute's Howard Husock writes of the days when communities of all types embraced that concept of a "'housing ladder' – a spectrum of housing affordable to all types of buyers and renters that facilitated upward mobility and reduced energy consumption."[69] We need to rediscover that concept.

In 2015, California's Legislative Analyst's Office examined the causes of the state's high housing costs: "On top of the 100,000 to 140,000 housing units California is expected to build each year, the state would probably have to as many as 100,000 additional units annually – almost exclusively in its coastal communities – to seriously mitigate its problems with housing affordability." In 2021, the state built fewer than 113,000 new units of all types, according to the state Department of Finance. It's all about housing construction, period.[70]

Finally, some of California's Democratic officials have recognized that the crisis is ultimately a supply problem, but they have approached it in the usual regulatory way – by imposing housing plans on localities. Liberal communities in Marin County and conservative cities in the Inland Empire continue to battle the state over how many new housing units they must permit.[71] Apparently, NIMBYism (Not In My Back Yard) is a bipartisan movement.

The good news is the Legislature enacted two promising new laws, Senate Bills 9 and 10, which take a market-oriented approach toward housing construction. As the group California YIMBY (Yes In My Back Yard) notes, state government makes it largely illegal to build middle-class, multi-family housing in 70 percent of the state. SB 9 allows homeowners to subdivide their lots – and to build two units on each lot. SB 10 enables cities to permit projects up to 10 units on infill sites and along transit corridors.[72]

Instead of having to go tail-between-the-legs to city bureaucrats and planning commissions to get approvals based on subjective criteria, owners now have the right to build provided they meet established regulatory standards. The new law also exempts projects from the onerous requirements of the California Environmental Quality Act or CEQA, which encourages project opponents to file costly and time-delaying lawsuits against virtually any proposed project.

I also see SB 9 as a great pro-family measure.[73] In the Sacramento exurb where I live, property owners have long had the right to build a second home up to 1,000 square feet on our small acreages. They mostly build tasteful second units to house adult children and elderly parents. Many older cities have homes on big lots that are ripe for SB 9 upgrades. SB 10 will boost the development of condominiums in densely populated but underutilized neighborhoods.

However encouraging these new laws may be, they only boost supply around the margins given their limited nature. After all, few homeowners are going to subdivide their lot and essentially play housing developer and speculator. Western states need more such reforms. In Oregon, for instance, lawmakers removed single-family-only zoning, meaning that developers can build duplexes throughout the state. Counter to misrepresentations, that new law does not ban the construction of single-family homes. It only bans a form of zoning that requires the construction of such homes.[74]

The recent interest-rate hikes are causing a rapid slowdown in the housing market.[75] We'll soon see if prices begin to moderate or even fall, but the West's housing problems have been brewing for years – and the solution requires a long-term commitment to boosting supply. That will be a boon for cities, which can once again be magnets for people at all income levels and all family situations.

Reviving Urban Schools Will Revive Cities

WHEN MY WIFE AND I moved to Southern California in the late 1990s, we rented a small house in Fullerton for nearly a year. Then we began the disheartening process of finding a house that we could afford. We left one of the nation's least-expensive metro areas (current median price: $155,000) for one of the least-affordable areas (current median price: $1,020,000).[76]

We found a nice bungalow in Anaheim's historic Colony District, an urban neighborhood that was similar to settled old neighborhoods where we lived in the Midwest. But we faced two challenges. My wife (rightly) conditioned our move to California on my promise that we'd be able to own a single-family house with a yard. It didn't need to be big or fancy, but she wanted a real house and not a condo or apartment. Second, our three kids were young, so we needed to move into a decent school district, which was quite a challenge at lower price points.

Whenever we found a house that might work, we called the principal of the local school to assess the educational situation – and we checked a database that posted test scores and ratings of the local schools. I still recall talking to one principal who said that, frankly, his school couldn't meet our kids' needs because almost all of the students were non-English speakers and from extremely poor households. There were few gifted programs and extracurricular activities. He recommended we look elsewhere. We ended up moving to a suburban district with stellar test scores, but the experience reminded me of the crucial role that schools play in home selection.[77]

The 2015 National Association of Realtors Home Buyer and Seller Generational Trends study found that homebuyers placed the "quality of the school district" as its sixth-highest criteria for choosing a home – a number that was fourth-highest for people in prime child-rearing ages."[78] I'm genuinely surprised that school quality didn't rank first or second.

Imagine the urban revitalization we'd see if all parents had access to quality charter schools. We couldn't afford private schools on top of our mortgage. However, if quality charters were readily available, we still could have considered that neighborhood. Anaheim had charters at the time, but demand exceeded supply – and school districts were strict about inter-district transfers. That's why school choice is so important – to improve student performance and make urban living possible for young families.

"American cities are becoming more and more unfriendly to families, and new parents are fleeing for the exurbs, where housing is more affordable and schools are better," according to a report in *Axios*. The share of school-age children is dropping dramatically in cities nationwide, with big cities becoming like a barbell, as one urban demographer noted, with large populations of young professionals on one end and wealthy empty nesters on the other.[79]

San Francisco and Seattle have the lowest populations of households with children (16.5 percent and 18.7 percent, respectively) and Portland, Ore., isn't far behind (23.2 percent).[80] San Francisco has widely been termed a childless city. Cost of living issues play a key role, but so do educational opportunities. That's why San Francisco's school-board recall is so encouraging. It's a sign that local parents might be pushing back against the unions and ideologues who seem uninterested in educational excellence.

School choice does help neighborhoods values. After a Dallas-area school district (Edgewood) embraced a voucher program, property values flourished. "Conservative estimates based on two sets of 'control' districts found that the voucher program had significant positive impacts on single- and multi-family housing numbers and market value," according to a study published by the University of Texas-San Antonio.[81] Statistics aside, educational choice is good for cities and urban neighborhoods.

Although the higher courts later overturned the ruling, the 2014 *Vergara* decision highlighted the never-ending struggles in California's public schools. Los Angeles Superior Court Judge Rolf Treu tossed aside the state's teacher tenure and dismissal statutes because they kept ineffective teachers in the classroom and thereby deprived students of their constitutional right to a quality education. (His ruling was overturned on appeal.) Treu said the testimony showing the large number of kids who are permanently scarred by poor teachers "shocked the conscience."[82] Urban schools suffer the most given that they often become the dumping ground for teachers who ought not to be in the classroom.

Yet nothing ever changes. "Since 2008 … California has initiated sweeping reforms in an attempt to channel more resources to high-needs students and to better level the educational playing field," according to a 2020 report in *CALMatters*. "Black, Latino and poor students still lag dramatically behind Asian American, white and wealthier students."[83] Major cash infusions haven't helped, and the state is placing stricter limits on charter expansions.

"There are many reasons for the decline of America's cities, but one of the key reasons why many families flee older urban areas is because of the poor quality of city public schools," my Pacific Research Institute colleague Lance Izumi concluded in a Free Cities Center report. "Research has shown, however, that one way to reverse this flight is to implement effective school choice programs."[84] It's past time for Western officials to heed that advice.

Getting the Crime Problem Under Control

ONE OF THE MOST encouraging political trends in recent years had been the generally bipartisan movement to reform the criminal-justice system.

Liberals had long championed revamping the bail system, diversion programs to keep young offenders from entering the justice system, and alternatives to incarceration. Conservative groups like Right on Crime – backed by Newt Gingrich, Grover Norquist, Ed Messe, Rick Perry and other Republican stalwarts – then joined the movement and pushed the discussion toward helping nonviolent offenders while keeping dangerous people behind bars.[85]

That's a sensible and balanced approach, and one that had widespread public support during a time of falling crime rates. In 2019, the nation's murder rate had dropped to five per 100,000 people – lower than the 5.1 rate in 1960 and half of the peak in 1980. Violent crime of all types had fallen to 379 per 100,000 people, completing a long and steady drop since a peak of 732 in 1990.[86] Likewise, property crimes had fallen virtually in half since the 1980 peak. California tracked the national statistics

– with somewhat higher violent crime rates and property crime rates, but lower murder rates.[87]

But amidst the COVID-19 shutdowns and riots following the George Floyd killing in Minneapolis, nationwide homicide rates jumped almost 30 percent in 2020, according to a report in the Council on Criminal Justice.[88]

In California, property crime rates in its largest cities spiked dramatically, but then settled back to historic levels – despite high-profile smash-and-grab robberies, according to data analyzed by the Public Policy Institute of California.[89] Yet auto-theft rates soared statewide by 19 percent in 2020, and homicide and aggravated assaults also went up. The state's homicide-rate increase matched the 30-percent increase nationwide – and rates shot up even in rural counties.

The situation in California and other Western states isn't appreciably different from other states, which certainly should give pause to those who wholly blame California-specific policies (such as Proposition 47,[90] which treated many nonviolent crimes as misdemeanors rather than felonies). Those policies deserve scrutiny. They have led to various problems, but they might not be the source of the overall crime spike. Westerners, especially those living in urban areas, feel unsafe and are upset by a growing sense of disorder. Such discontent is creating political waves.

"California jurisdictions with some of the harshest prosecutors – like Riverside – have the highest crime rates. And violent crime in California is worse in conservative jurisdictions," argued San Francisco's assistant district attorney Rachel Marshall in a May column in the *San Francisco Chronicle*.[91] That's largely correct, but politics is about narratives, not data. Californians are tired of crime – and they are blaming those responsible for prosecuting it.

Even in liberal Oregon, the story is the same. A May 2022 Oregon Public Broadcasting (OPB) poll found that homelessness topped voters' lists of concerns with "safety, crime, policing" coming in third.[92]

OPB notes that, "In the Portland metro area, homicides have soared in recent years. Portland tallied 91 homicides in 2021, shattering a record set in 1987. The number of shootings in Portland has also tripled since 2019, shining a spotlight on a very violent and visible crime indicator."[93] Given this, it shouldn't be surprising that voters are reacting to that "very violent and visible" indicator.

Even during relatively low crime periods, politicians have exploited fears to win votes. Ronald Reagan was elected California governor in 1966 on a tough-on-crime platform. Crime rates had edged up since the early 1960s but remained relatively low at the time of his campaign. Despite California's reputation as a bastion of progressivism, its voters have frequently supported tough-on-crime initiatives – including the nation's most stringent three-strikes-and-you're-out law. In the 1998 governor's race, both candidates fought over who would be the toughest – with Democrat Gray Davis vowing to execute offenders as young as age 14. Crime rates then were at their peak.[94]

Since 2011, California began moving in a more reform-minded direction. Facing a prison-overcrowding crisis and federal court mandates to reduce the population, then-Gov. Jerry Brown enacted a "realignment" law that reduced overcrowding by moving inmates to county jails. In 2012, voters amended the 1994 three-strikes law so that only a serious third strike would result in a life term. In 2014, voters enacted the afore-mentioned Proposition 47, followed by Proposition 57 in 2016, which increased the use of parole rather than incarceration. Now the pendulum is swinging back in a tough-on-crime direction, although it remains to be seen whether any such efforts will reach the ballot. The last justice-related ballot measures would have eliminated the death penalty and cash bail – but both failed.[95]

Crime remains the central issue in urban policy for obvious reasons. We can't revive cities and entice new families to move to them if people don't feel safe on the streets or in their homes. We can embrace thoughtful reforms to the justice system and take a hard line on serious crime at the same time.

There's little evidence that sensible criminal-justice reforms are behind the increase in crime. Holding accountable misbe-having police officers enhances public safety, which depends in part on the trust between police officers and the citizens they're sworn to protect and serve. Law-enforcement budgets deserve the same scrutiny as any other department. No agency should be off limits to a sharpened pencil.

Nevertheless, the public is right to be outraged at the pro-gressive approach that views all criminals as victims of soci-ety and discriminatory police practices – and refuses to make distinctions between nonviolent offenders and predators who endanger law-abiding citizens. Keeping young nonviolent offenders out of the justice system and releasing repeat offenders are two different matters.

As the *Orange County Register* explained in an editorial following the Boudin recall, "It's laudable to seek alternatives to incarceration, stop overcharging defendants, provide low-level criminals with treatment options, only charge juveniles as adults for violent crimes, hold misbehaving police officers accountable and to try to put 'justice' back into the justice system. But prosecutors can at the same time take a hard line against violent predators, street crime and public disorder."[96]

Elected officials embracing a balanced approach offer the best hope for restoring safe communities.

The Next Phase for Urban Renewal

BECAUSE OF GROWING SLUM conditions in many of the nation's largest cities, the federal government passed the Housing Act of 1949, which sparked decades of urban-renewal projects across the country. According to the federal Housing and Urban Development Department, the act "declares that the general welfare and security of the nation requires the establishment of a national housing policy to realize, as soon as feasible, the goal of a decent home and a suitable living environment for every American family." It also "authorizes federal advances, loans, and grants to localities to assist slum clearance and urban redevelopment."[97]

The results were often the opposite of what lawmakers promised. Instead of building decent homes for every American, state and local governments used vast new eminent-domain powers to demolish neighborhoods and replace them with public projects.

Resulting public-housing projects often became breeding grounds for crime, poverty and despair – and they always were woefully mismanaged. Some of these disastrous, modernist housing flops are known by their names – Pruitt-Igoe in St. Louis, Cabrini-Green in Chicago, Magnolia Projects in New

Orleans and Jordan Downs in Los Angeles.[98] The end result should have been predicted.

"Socialized shelter in this country is perpetually in disrepair, shoddily managed and actively harmful to the well-being of tenants while doing little to integrate residents into their economy or community," notes the Manhattan Institute's Michael Hendrix.[99]

These projects primarily shifted resources away from housing, as cities cleared away slum neighborhoods and provided the remaining parcels to major developers. Cities found it much more lucrative to build commercial buildings and high rises, while relegating the "projects" to distant neighborhoods disconnected from jobs and shopping.

Most people think about older Eastern, Southern and Midwestern cities when they hear the term urban renewal, but officials embraced the same policies here on the West Coast. One of the best-known controversies involved Chavez Ravine. "During the early 1950s, the city of Los Angeles forcibly evicted the 300 families . . . to make way for a low-income public housing project," according to a PBS documentary.[100] Later, instead of building promised housing, the land was sold to Dodgers owner Walter O'Malley for a stadium site to facilitate the team's move from New York.

In the late 1940s, California created a statewide system of locally-controlled redevelopment agencies, which gave cities and counties the financing and eminent domain tools to regenerate languishing urban neighborhoods. Traditionally, cities could use their takings power for public uses, but they eventually wielded it on behalf of private developers – something that the U.S. Supreme Court upheld in its 2005 *Kelo v. New London* decision.[101]

In her dissent, the late Justice Sandra Day O'Connor captured the essence of what was wrong not only with the redevelopment process, but with most of the nation's urban-renewal efforts: "Any property may now be taken for the benefit of another private party, but the fallout from this decision will not be random. The beneficiaries are likely to be those citizens with disproportionate influence and power in the political process, including large corporations and development firms. As for the victims, the government now has license to transfer property from those with fewer resources to those with more."[102]

The key financial mechanism is something known as tax-increment financing. The local redevelopment agency would identify an area that needed improvement and deem it "blighted." (The definitions of blight were expansive – and consultants always found the required blight.) The agency could then float debt to pay for related infrastructure improvement – and cities would grab the increase in property taxes levied after the project was complete. The state required agencies to divert 20 percent of the tax increment on subsidized housing.

Like redevelopment's liberal eminent domain provisions, its broad financial rules also led to widespread abuse. For starters, local agencies – typically run by the City Council – could float debt without a vote of the public. The increment the agencies received came at the expense of traditional public agencies including police, fire and public schools. The state backfilled the school losses, which meant that redevelopment agencies eventually siphoned 13-percent of the state's general fund budget.

Most significantly, the agencies distorted local development decisions. Some cities invested in traditional urban renewal projects (e.g., Pasadena's Old Town and San Diego's Gaslamp Quarter), but mostly cities learned that they could use it as a tool to grab additional revenues from their respective counties. They typically subsidized big-box stores, hotels and auto malls – because those retail complexes provided oodles of discretionary sales-tax dollars.

I was among a politically heterogeneous group – including liberal U.S. Rep. Maxine Waters and conservative U.S. Rep. Tom McClintock – that sought restraints on the powers of these crony capitalist agencies. After *Kelo*, most states reformed their eminent domain laws at the suggestion of the Supreme Court majority. California voters ultimately passed a modest "reform" that was written by the pro-redevelopment California Redevelopment Association and the League of California Cities.[103]

In 2011, desperate for money to close a $30 billion deficit, Gov. Jerry Brown shuttered the state's redevelopment agencies.[104] Later, the Legislature created Infrastructure Finance Districts that re-imposed some tax-increment financing elements, but with far more restrictions. Cities still abuse eminent domain, but they've lost the incentive to do so routinely. The latest effort to bring back a version of redevelopment failed in the Legislature.[105]

Despite a few arguable successes, redevelopment agencies created vast harm in terms of actual urban renewal. They were far more competent at bulldozing historic areas, such as the demolition of Orange County's largest and most historic downtown in Anaheim in the 1970s, than rebuilding them. Anaheim's demolished downtown area has yet to fully recover.

It's worth noting that, in Sacramento, the one downtown street that has been most resistant to improvement is the centrally located K Street. That is the street where city officials have directed most of their attention. At first, they blocked off the street to road traffic, and then subsidized a variety of restaurants (including a Mermaid bar).[106] Officials let the private sector take the lead elsewhere downtown – an approach that has led to an energetic nightlife scene. Perhaps City Hall might one-day notice the connection. Government urban renewal is not the same thing as actual urban renewal. More of the former often restricts the latter. It's about time that urban officials throughout the country recognize that less oftentimes is more.

Building Better and Freer Cities

WESTERN CITIES REMAIN BASTIONS of innovative thinking and entrepreneurship, as epitomized by the booming tech, entertainment and biotech industries. Unfortunately, innovative ideas that promote competition – such as running small and maneuverable jitneys rather than lumbering buses – can never get off the ground because urban incentive structures are wrong.

To the latter example, no city manager would propose a plan that confronts the drivers' union. In 44 out of 50 major cities, public-transit use is falling – despite record subsidies and an all-out effort by policymakers to drive commuters out of their cars.[107] Perhaps if city officials focused more on making transit riding appealing, ridership would increase. No private enterprise would stay in business by taking that approach.

"(I)t is time to end subsidies to transit and consider privatizing it instead," wrote the libertarian Cato Institute's Randal O'Toole in 2020. "Private operators can provide transit at a lower cost than government agencies and will offer service that is responsive to transit riders, not political whims."[108] That may or may not be the right idea – but the Free Cities Center is devoted to exploring out-of-the box thinking that could improve urban life. At the very least, cities could find ways to bring market forces to bear on the provision of all types of services.

Budget issues are another area ripe for reform. Because of the power of public-sector unions in the biggest cities, municipal budgets spend too much on everything – from pension benefits to the construction of low-income housing. Government officials often tout how much they spend because it shows their commitment to a particular service. However, widespread misspending provides little bang for the buck.

When Anaheim's Councilman Tait created his Freedom Friendly City model, a core element was teaching the city's bureaucracy to take a more customer-oriented approach to its business rather than the typical bureaucratic approach. Cities often behave as if the citizens are their adversaries, and often quash their creative endeavors.[109] Here are two examples:

Residents of Philadelphia's Fishtown neighborhood planted a garden at a traffic circle to beautify it. In response, the city deemed the decorative rocks a hazard and announced a plan to remove them. "It's frustrating enough that the Streets Department can't pick up the trash, pave the streets, or, really, do anything competently," a local resident told the *Philadelphia Inquirer*.[110] The city can't manage its basic responsibilities, but it can harass residents who try to fill the gap.

St. Louis Public Radio reported this year on the late artist Bob Cassilly, who built a museum of sorts at an empty 600,000 square-foot shoe factory beginning in 1993. His project, which resembles an avant-garde jungle gym, is now a source of local pride. The artist had to defy building codes and constantly fight with city inspectors to get it done.[111] Los Angeles' Watts Towers, built in 1920, are considered a key architectural landmark – but could probably never be built under today's city rules.[112]

That's just a reminder that cities have become too rule bound, with planning officials overly committed to controlling every development and land use within their boundaries. The Free Cities Center will examine every manner of urban issue, but our resounding goal is clear. Let's free urban residents to live better and more interesting lives.

Endnotes

1   Mary Procter, *Gritty Cities: A second look at Allentown, Bethlehem, Bridge-port, Hoboken, Lancaster, Norwich, Paterson, Reading, Trenton, Troy, Water-bury, Wilmington*, 1978, Temple University Press. https://www.amazon.com/Gritty-Cities-Mary-Procter/dp/087722143X

2   Wolf Von Eckardt, "Gritty Cities," *The Washington Post*, Dec. 9, 1978, https://www.washingtonpost.com/archive/lifestyle/1978/12/09/gritty-cities/eee4ea64-7833-4471-bb6d-4d375e6b0fd5/

3   Kevin Klinkenberg, "What is a 'messy' city?" *The Messy City Blog*, Jan. 8, 2022, https://www.kevinklinkenberg.com/blog/what-is-a-messy-city

4   Jane Jacobs, *The Death and Life of Great American Cities*, 1961, Vintage Books, Page 188, https://www.buurtwijs.nl/sites/default/files/buurtwijs/bestanden/jane_jacobs_the_death_and_life_of_great_american.pdf

5   Kevin Klinkenberg, "What is a 'messy' city?" *The Messy City Blog*, Jan. 8, 2022, https://www.kevinklinkenberg.com/blog/what-is-a-messy-city

6   Kerry Jackson, "First thing we do, let's retrain all the planners," *Free Cities Center*, Forthcoming issue.

7   Roger K. Lewis, "Architectural failures, flaws and foul-ups," *The Washington Post*, June 19, 1993, https://www.washingtonpost.com/archive/realestate/1993/06/19/architectural-failures-flaws-and-foul-ups/6d-48ca97-5b1c-4ce2-9ea1-7e1aa706ff9f/

8   Tony Bizjak, "City of Sacramento considering new set of 'road diets'," *Sacramento Bee*, May 1, 2015, https://www.sacbee.com/news/local/transportation/back-seat-driver/article19985379.html

9   Timothy B. Lee, "Before-and-after maps show how freeways transformed America's cities," *Vox*, June 19, 2016, https://www.vox.com/2014/12/29/7460557/urban-freeway-slider-maps

10   Kevin Kruse, *White Flight: Atlanta and the Making of Modern Conservatism*, 2005, Princeton University Press, https://www.amazon.com/White-Flight-Atlanta-Conservatism-Politics/dp/0691133867

11   Cleveland Rogers, "Robert Moses: A Portrait," *Atlantic*, February 1939, https://www.theatlantic.com/magazine/archive/1939/02/robert-moses/306543/

12   Ibid.

13   *Redevelopment: The Unknown Government*, Municipal Officials for Redevelopment Reform, September 2007, https://cotce.ca.gov/meetings/testimony/documents/CHRIS%20NORBY%20-%20ATTACH.PDF

14   Mindy Fullilove, *Root Shock: How Tearing Up City Neighborhoods Hurts America, and What We Can Do About It*, 2004, New York University Press, https://www.worldcat.org/title/root-shock-how-tearing-up-city-neighborhoods-hurts-america-and-what-we-can-do-about-it/oclc/53970697

15   Ibid.

16   "The godfather of sprawl," *Atlantic*, December 2007, https://www.theatlantic.com/magazine/archive/2007/12/the-godfather-of-sprawl/306542/

17   Jane Jacobs, *The Death and Life of Great American Cities*, 1961, Vintage Books, Page 188, https://www.buurtwijs.nl/sites/default/files/buurtwijs/bestanden/jane_jacobs_the_death_and_life_of_great_american.pdf

18   Ibid., p. 15

19   Ibid., p. 24

20   Sean Miller, "Snapcrap – Why I built an app to report poop on the streets of San Francisco," *Medium*, Jan. 5, 2019, https://medium.com/@miller.stowe/snapcrap-why-i-built-an-app-to-report-poop-on-the-streets-of-san-francisco-aac12382a7ce#:~:text=app%20it%20deserved.-,The%20App,if%20they%20have%20been%20resolved

21   Michael R. Blood, "LA spending up to $837,000 to house a single homeless person," Associated Press, Feb. 23, 2022, https://abcnews.go.com/Politics/wireStory/la-spending-837000-house-single-homeless-person-83072411

22   Todd Spitzer, "Don't let OC become another LA with Gascón-like policies," *The Orange County Register*, March 9, 2022, https://www.ocregister.com/2022/03/09/dont-let-oc-become-another-la-with-gascon-like-policies-todd-spitzer/

23   Jenny Goldsberry, "Los Angeles County district attorney backpedals on criminal justice reforms," *Washington Examiner*, Feb. 19, 2022, https://www.washingtonexaminer.com/restoring-america/fairness-justice/los-angeles-county-district-attorney-backpedals-on-criminal-justice-reforms

24   Sean Miller, "Snapcrap – Why I built an app to report poop on the streets of San Francisco," *Medium*, Jan. 5, 2019, https://medium.com/@miller.stowe/snapcrap-why-i-built-an-app-to-report-poop-on-the-streets-of-san-francisco-aac12382a7ce#:~:text=app%20it%20deserved.-,The%20App,if%20they%20have%20been%20resolved

25   Michael Shellenberger, *San Fransicko: Why Progressives Ruin Cities*, Harper, Oct. 12, 2021, https://www.amazon.com/San-Fransicko-Progressives-Ruin-Cities/dp/0063093626

26   Steven Greenhut, "California politicians push urbanism, as people flee cities," *The Orange County Register*, April 7, 2022, https://www.ocregister.com/2022/04/07/california-politicians-push-urbanism-as-people-flee-cities/

27   Shawn Chitnis, "San Francisco post-pandemic population drop steepest among major U.S. cities," CBS News, May 26, 2022, https://www.cbsnews.com/sanfrancisco/news/san-francisco-post-pandemic-population-drop-steepest-among-major-us-cities/#:~:text=From%20April%201%2C%202020%20to,same%20level%20as%20San%20Francisco

28   KING 5 Staff, "Dept. of Justice deems Seattle an 'anarchist jurisdiction' for CHOP zone," KING 5 NBC Seattle, Sept. 21, 2020, https://www.king5.com/article/news/politics/dept-of-justice-says-seattle-is-permitting-violence-and-destruction-of-property/281-d84f74a7-c27f-402e-9720-07a46cccb957

29   Vanessa Romo, "San Francisco School Board Rescinds Controversial School Renaming Plan," KQED, April 7, 2021, https://www.npr.org/2021/04/07/984919925/san-francisco-school-board-rescinds-controversial-school-renaming-plan

30   Faith Pinho, "Contentious George Washington mural at San Francisco school can stay, judge decides," *Los Angeles Times*, July 28, 2021, https://www.latimes.com/california/story/2021-07-28/contentious-george-washington-mural-at-san-francisco-school-can-stay-judge-decides

31 Thomas Fuller, "'You Have to Give Us Respect': How Asian Americans Fueled the San Francisco Recall," *The New York Times*, Feb. 17, 2022, https://www.nytimes.com/2022/02/17/us/san-francisco-school-board-parents.html

32 Catherine Kim, "San Francisco mayor on the school board recall: 'We failed our children'," *Politico*, Feb. 20, 2022, https://www.politico.com/news/2022/02/20/san-francisco-mayor-school-board-recall-00010392

33 Musadiq Bidar, "San Francisco votes overwhelmingly to recall progressive DA Chesa Boudin," June 8, 2022, https://www.cbsnews.com/news/chesa-boudin-san-francisco-da-recalled/

34 "Chesa Boudin Recall," Ballotpedia, Accessed June 25, 2022, https://ballotpedia.org/Chesa_Boudin_recall,_San_Francisco,_California_(2021-2022)#cite_note-7

35 Tony Saavedra, "OC District Attorney Todd Spitzer on way to win, looks for 'common ground,'" *The Orange County Register*, June 8, 2022, https://www.ocregister.com/2022/06/08/oc-district-attorney-todd-spitzer-on-way-to-win-looks-for-common-ground/

36 David French, "In San Francisco, Reason Beats Radicalism," *The Atlantic* newsletter (*The Third Rail*), Feb. 17, 2022, https://newsletters.theatlantic.com/the-third-rail/620e80ef6c908600204e3821/a-victory-for-the-exhausted-majority-in-san-francisco/

37 Spencer Custodio and Hassam Elattar, "Anaheim Mayor Harry Sidhu Resigns After FBI Reveals Anaheim Corruption Probe," *Voice of OC*, May 23, 2022, https://voiceofoc.org/2022/05/anaheim-mayor-harry-sidhu-resigns-after-fbi-reveals-anaheim-corruption-probe/

38 Curt Pringle, "A Bias Towards Freedom: Freedom Breeds: Choice and Innovation in Anaheim," *Innovators In Action*, Reason Foundation, no date, https://www.scottsdaleaz.gov/AssetFactory.aspx?did=30720

39 Meghan Henry, Tanya de Sousa, Caroline Roddey, et al., "The 2020 Annual Homeless Assessment Report (AHAR) to Congress," U.S. Department of Housing and Urban Development, January 2021 https://www.huduser.gov/portal/sites/default/files/pdf/2020-AHAR-Part-1.pdf

40   Lauren Hepler, Sarah Ravani, Yoohyun Jung, "Homelessness surged 35% in one Bay Area county. Here's what new data for each region reveals," *San Francisco Chronicle*, May 16, 2022, https://www.sfchronicle.com/bayarea/article/Homeless-populations-surge-11-in-San-Jose-and-8-17176329.php

41   Staff, "A Snapshot of Homeless Californians in Shelters," Blog post, Public Policy Institute of California, March 2, 2022, https://www.ppic.org/blog/a-snapshot-of-homeless-californians-in-shelters/

42   Gary Warth, "Homeless count up 10% in San Diego County. 'More miserable out there than I have seen in years,'" *San Diego Union-Tribune*, May 19, 2022, https://www.sandiegouniontribune.com/news/homelessness/story/2022-05-19/despite-more-shelters-outreach-programs-homelessness-on-rise-in-san-diego

43   Chris Nichols, "Sacramento's homeless population spikes 67% to nearly 9,300 since 2019," Capitol Public Radio, June 28, 2022, https://www.capradio.org/articles/2022/06/28/sacramentos-homeless-population-spikes-67-to-nearly-9300-since-2019/#:~:text=Since%202019%2C%20Sacramento%20County's%20homeless,and%20now%209%2C278%20in%202022.

44   Interview with author, May 2022

45   Jason M. Ward, Rick Garvey, Sarah B. Hunter, *Recent Trends Among the Unsheltered in Three Los Angeles Neighborhoods*, RAND Corp., 2022, https://www.rand.org/pubs/research_reports/RRA1890-1.html

46   Benjamin Oreskes and Doug Smith, "Many homeless people resist group shelters even as L.A. mayoral candidates push to build more," *Los Angeles Times*, May 4, 2022, https://www.latimes.com/homeless-housing/story/2022-05-04/as-mayoral-candidates-call-for-expansion-of-shelter-homeless-people-want-none-of-it

47   Ibid.

48   Staff, "Housing First," California Housing and Community Development agency website, Accessed June 25, 2022, https://www.hcd.ca.gov/grants-funding/active-funding/docs/housing-first-fact-sheet.pdf

49   Judge Glock, "Housing First is a Failure," Cicero Institute, Jan. 13, 2022, https://ciceroinstitute.org/research/housing-first-is-a-failure/

50 Interview with author, May 2022

51 Staff, "California Care Court," California Department of Health and Human Services fact sheet, Accessed June 25, 2022, https://www.chhs.ca.gov/care-court/

52 "Proposition 47: The Safe Neighborhoods and Schools Act," California Courts overview, https://www.courts.ca.gov/prop47.htm

53 Disability Rights California coalition, "Disability Rights California & Coalition's Letter in Opposition to CARE Court," May 11, 2022, https://www.disabilityrightsca.org/latest-news/disability-rights-california-coalitions-letter-in-opposition-to-care-court

54 Ibid.

55 Jocelyn Wiener, "Breakdown: California's mental health system, explained," *CAL Matters*, April 30, 2019, https://calmatters.org/explainers/breakdown-californias-mental-health-system-explained/

56 Ryan Lillis, "Map shows the median home value in every state. California's ranking might surprise you," *Sacramento Bee*, March 9, 2022, https://www.sacbee.com/news/business/real-estate-news/article259193628.html

57 Mark Strassman, "The least affordable housing market in the U.S.? Boise," CBS News, Dec. 23, 2021, https://www.cbsnews.com/news/housing-market-boise-idaho-least-affordable/#:~:text=Boise%2C%20Idaho%20%E2%80%94%20Boise%20is%20having,in%20Boise%20dwarf%20residents'%20incomes

58 "County Median Home Prices and Monthly Mortgage Payment," National Association of Realtors, https://www.nar.realtor/research-and-statistics/housing-statistics/county-median-home-prices-and-monthly-mortgage-payment

59 Ibid.

60 Realtor.com search, Punxsutawney, Pa., https://www.realtor.com/realestateandhomes-search/Punxsutawney_PA

61 Zillow and Inflation Calculator

62 California Association of Realtors, "Housing Affordability Index," Accessed June 25, 2022, https://www.car.org/marketdata/data/haitraditional

63 Ibid.

64 Megan McArdle, "The one issue every economist can agree is bad: Rent control," *The Washington Post*, June 14, 2019, https://www.washingtonpost.com/opinions/2019/06/15/comeback-rent-control-just-time-make-housing-shortages-worse/

65 "Homeownership," The Urban Institute, Accessed June 25, 2022, https://www.urban.org/tags/homeownership

66 Ibid.

67 Whitney Airgood-Obrycki, "COVID-19 will delay housing construction, but for how long?" Joint Center for Housing Studies of Harvard University, May 7, 2020, https://www.jchs.harvard.edu/blog/covid-19-will-delay-housing-construction-but-for-how-long

68 "Urban growth boundary," Oregon Metro, Accessed June 25, 2022, https://www.oregonmetro.gov/urban-growth-boundary

69 Howard Husock, "Building a Housing Ladder: Lessons from, and for, Silicon Valley," *City Journal*, Oct. 3, 2018, https://www.manhattan-institute.org/html/urban-policy-2018-building-housing-ladder-lessons-silicon-valley-11511.html

70 Mac Taylor, "California's High Housing Costs: Causes and Consequences," Legislative Analyst's Office, March 17, 2015, https://lao.ca.gov/reports/2015/finance/housing-costs/housing-costs.aspx

71 Nigel Duara, "Wealthy Southern California Cities Fight Affordable Housing Mandates," *CAL Matters*, Jan 2, 2021, https://timesofsandiego.com/politics/2021/01/02/wealthy-southern-california-cities-fight-affordable-housing-mandates/

72 Staff, "SB 9," California YIMBY, Accessed June 25, 2022, https://cayimby.org/sb-9/

73 Steven Greenhut, "Land-use bill promotes freedom and property rights," *The Orange County Register*, Aug. 27, 2021, https://www.ocregister.com/2021/08/27/land-use-bill-promotes-freedom-and-property-rights/

74   Julia Shumway, "White House: Oregon single-family zoning law could be model for nation," *Oregon Capital Chronicle*, Oct. 29, 2021, https://oregoncapitalchronicle.com/2021/10/29/white-house-oregon-single-family-zoning-law-could-be-model-for-nation/#:~:text=By%3A%20 Julia%20Shumway%20%2D%20October%2029%2C%202021%20 4%3A30%20pm&text=Oregon's%202019%20law%20effectively%20 ending,Kotek%2C%20who%20spearheaded%20the%20law

75   Giulia Carbonaro, "Are We Heading for a Housing Market Crash? What Home Sales Data Reveals," *Newsweek*, June 24, 2022, https://www.newsweek.com/heading-housing-market-crash-what-home-sales-data-reveals-american-economy-1718863

76   Zillow comparison of Lima, Ohio, with Orange County, Calif.

77   California School Ratings website, https://school-ratings.com/

78   Research Division, *Home Buyer and Seller Generational Trends Report 2015*, National Association of Realtors, March 2015 https://www.nar.realtor/sites/default/files/reports/2015/2015-home-buyer-and-seller-generational-trends-2015-03-11.pdfl

79   Erica Pandey, "The great family exodus," *Axios*, Oct. 30, 2018, https://www.axios.com/2018/10/30/families-children-cities-san-francisco-housing-prices

80   Ibid.

81   John Merrifield, Nathan Gray et al, "An Evaluation of the CEO Horizon, 1998-2008, Edgewood Tuition Voucher Program," University of Texas-San Antonio, Aug. 31, 2009, http://faculty.business.utsa.edu/jmerrifi/evp.pdf

82   *Vergara v. California*, California Court of Appeal, April 14, 2016, 246 Cal. App. 4th 619; Docket No. B258589S (Cal. Ct. App. 2016), https://law.justia.com/cases/california/court-of-appeal/2016/b258589.html

83   Richard Cano and Joe Hong, "Mind the achievement gap: California's disparities in education, explained," *CAL Matters*, Feb. 3, 2020, https://calmatters.org/explainers/achievement-gap-california-explainer-schools-education-disparities-explained/

84   Lance Izumi, "Want to save cities? Then revamp urban schools," *Free Cities Center*, Forthcoming issue.

85 Statement of Principles, Right on Crime, https://rightoncrime.com/wp-content/uploads/2011/09/Statement-of-Principles.pdf

86 Crime data, Uniform Crime Reporting Program, FBI, https://www.fbi.gov/services/cjis/ucr

87 Magnus Lofstrom and Brandon Martin, "Crime Trends in California," Public Policy Institute of California, January 2022, https://www.ppic.org/publication/crime-trends-in-california/#:~:text=The%20state-wide%20property%20crime%20rate,ranked%2018th%20among%20all%20states

88 Dora Mekouar, "Why Homicide Rates in US Spiked 30% During COVID Pandemic," Voice of America, Feb. 2, 2022, https://www.voanews.com/a/why-homicide-rates-spiked-30-during-the-pandemic-/6420391.html

89 Magnus Lofstrom and Brandon Martin, "Crime Trends in California," Public Policy Institute of California, January 2022, https://www.ppic.org/publication/crime-trends-in-california/#:~:text=The%20state-wide%20property%20crime%20rate,ranked%2018th%20among%20all%20states

90 "Proposition 47: The Safe Neighborhoods and Schools Act," California Courts overview, https://www.courts.ca.gov/prop47.htm

91 Rachel Marshall, "The California crime discourse is all wrong," *San Francisco Chronicle*, May 26, 2022, https://www.sfgate.com/politics-op-eds/article/California-crime-discourse-is-wrong-17195276.php

92 Jonathan Levinson, "Some Oregon midterm candidates focus on crime – even when the data disagrees," Oregon Public Radio, April 21, 2022, https://www.opb.org/article/2022/04/21/oregon-governors-race-portland-city-council-crime-polling-data/

93 Ibid.

94 Steven Greenhut, "How California Softened its Tough-on-Crime Stance," R Street Institute Policy Paper, July 2017, https://www.rstreet.org/wp-content/uploads/2017/07/102.pdf

95 Ibid.

96   The Editorial Board, "Criminal justice reform isn't dead after Chesa Boudin's recall," *The Orange County Register*, June 11, 2022, https://www.oc-register.com/2022/06/11/criminal-justice-reform-isnt-dead-after-chesa-boudins-recall/

97   "Major Legislation on Housing and Urban Development Enacted Since 1931," U.S. Department of Housing and Urban Development, Accessed June 25, 2022, https://www.hud.gov/sites/documents/LEGS_CHRON_JUNE2014.PDF

98   Staff, "The 7 Most Infamous U.S. Public Housing Projects," *NewsOne*, Sept. 29, 2011, https://newsone.com/1555245/most-infamous-public-housing-projects/

99   Michael Hendrix, "America's failed experiment in public housing," *Governing*, May 10, 2021, https://www.governing.com/community/americas-failed-experiment-in-public-housing

100 Jordan Mechner, "Chavez Ravine: A Los Angeles Story," PBS, June 7, 2005, https://www.pbs.org/independentlens/documentaries/chavezravine/

101 *Kelo v. City of New London*, 545 U.S. 469 (2005), https://supreme.justia.com/cases/federal/us/545/469/#:~:text=City%20of%20New%20London%2C%20545%20U.S.%20469%20(2005)&text=Economic%20benefits%20are%20a%20permissible,seizing%20property%20from%20private%20citizens.

102 Ilya Somin, "The case against the Kelo decision – Part I," *Washington Post*, June 1, 2015, https://www.washingtonpost.com/news/volokh-conspiracy/wp/2015/06/01/why-the-kelo-decision-is-wrong-part-i/

103 Timothy Sandefur, "California Eminent Domain Reform is Now Prop. 98," Pacific Legal Foundation blog, Feb. 10, 2008, https://pacificlegal.org/california-eminent-domain-reform-is-now-prop-98/

104 Kendall Taggart, "Explainer: The end of redevelopment agencies," *The San Diego Union-Tribune*, Jan. 31, 2012, https://www.sandiegouniontribune.com/sdut-explainer-the-end-of-redevelopment-agencies-2012jan31-htmlstory.html

105 Timothy Coyle, "SB 5 is a wrong-headed re-make of redevelopment law," *PublicCEO*, Aug. 30, 2019, https://www.publicceo.com/2019/08/commentary-sb-5-is-a-wrong-headed-re-make-of-redevelopment-law/

106 George Skelton, "California's budget crisis a chance to rethink redevelopment funds," *Los Angeles Times*, Feb. 21, 2011, https://www.latimes.com/local/la-xpm-2011-feb-21-la-me-cap-redevelopment-20110221-story.html

107 Randal O'Toole, "Charting public transit's decline," Cato Institute, Nov. 8, 2018, https://www.cato.org/policy-analysis/charting-public-transits-decline

108 Randal O'Toole, "Transit: The Urban Parasite," Cato Institute, April 20, 2020, https://www.cato.org/policy-analysis/transit-urban-parasite

109 Steven Greenhut, "Mayor on right path in Anaheim," *The Orange County Register*, Aug. 4, 2012, https://www.ocregister.com/2012/08/04/steven-greenhut-mayor-on-right-path-in-anaheim/

110 Thomas Fitzgerald, "Landscaping of Fishtown roundabout a safety hazard," *Philadelphia Inquirer*, May 12, 2022, https://www.inquirer.com/transportation/streets-department-fishtown-roundabout-gardeners-rocks-20220512.html

111 Kayla Drake, "How City Museum defied building codes to become a St. Louis landmark," St. Louis Public Radio, May 12, 2022, https://news.stlpublicradio.org/show/st-louis-on-the-air/2022-05-12/how-city-museum-defied-building-codes-to-become-a-st-louis-landmark

112 California Department of Parks and Recreation, "Watts Towers of Simon Rodia State Historic Park," https://www.parks.ca.gov/?page_id=613

About the Author

STEVEN GREENHUT is a longtime journalist who has covered California politics since 1998. He wrote this book for the San Francisco-based Pacific Research Institute, where he founded that think tank's Sacramento-based journalism center in 2009. He currently is western region director for the R Street Institute, a Washington, D.C.-based free-market think tank, and is on the editorial board of the Southern California News Group. Greenhut has worked fulltime as a columnist for the *Orange County Register* and the *San Diego Union-Tribune*. He writes weekly for *American Spectator* and *Reason* magazines. He is the editor of *Saving California,* and the author of *Winning the Water Wars, Abuse of Power* and *Plunder.* He lives with his wife, Donna, on an acreage outside Sacramento and has three adult daughters.

About Pacific Research Institute

The Pacific Research Institute (PRI) champions freedom, opportunity, and personal responsibility by advancing free-market policy solutions. It provides practical solutions for the policy issues that impact the daily lives of all Americans, and demonstrates why the free market is more effective than the government at providing the important results we all seek: good schools, quality health care, a clean environment, and a robust economy.

Founded in 1979 and based in San Francisco, PRI is a non-profit, non-partisan organization supported by private contributions. Its activities include publications, public events, media commentary, community leadership, legislative testimony, and academic outreach.

Center for Business and Economics
PRI shows how the entrepreneurial spirit—the engine of economic growth and opportunity—is stifled by onerous taxes, regulations, and lawsuits. It advances policy reforms that promote a robust economy, consumer choice, and innovation.

Center for Education
PRI works to restore to all parents the basic right to choose the best educational opportunities for their children. Through research and grassroots outreach, PRI promotes parental choice in education, high academic standards, teacher quality, charter schools, and school-finance reform.

Center for the Environment
PRI reveals the dramatic and long-term trend toward a cleaner, healthier environment. It also examines and promotes the essential ingredients for abundant resources and environmental quality: property rights, markets, local action, and private initiative.

Center for Health Care
PRI demonstrates why a single-payer Canadian model would be detrimental to the health care of all Americans. It proposes market-based reforms that would improve affordability, access, quality, and consumer choice.

Center for California Reform
The Center for California Reform seeks to reinvigorate California's entrepreneurial self-reliant traditions. It champions solutions in education, business, and the environment that work to advance prosperity and opportunity for all the state's residents.

Center for Medical Economics and Innovation
The Center for Medical Economics and Innovation aims to educate policymakers, regulators, health care professionals, the media, and the public on the critical role that new technologies play in improving health and accelerating economic growth.

Free Cities Center
The Free Cities Center cultivates innovative ideas to improve our cities and urban life based around freedom and property rights – not government.